D1006013

FENG SHUI
FOR
DOGS

By Dogs, For Dogs

GERRY MAGUIRE
THOMPSON

GODSFIELD PRESS

Library of Congress Cataloging-in-Publication Data Available

10 9 8 7 6 5 4 3 2 1

Published in 1999 by Sterling Publishing Company, Inc.
387 Park Avenue South, New York, N.Y. 10016

© 1999 GODSFIELD PRESS
Text ©1999 Gerry Maguire Thompson

Distributed in Canada by Sterling Publishing
c/o Canadian Manda Group. One Atlantic Avenue, Suite 105
Toronto, Ontario, Canada M6K 3E7
Distributed in Australia by Capricorn Link (Australia) Pty Ltd
PO Box 6651, Baulkham Hills, Business Centre, NSW 2135, Australia

Printed and bound in Hong Kong

Sterling ISBN 0-8069-3148-5

CONTENTS

A SHAGGY DOG STORY

pot was in a real mess. He had poor appetite, low self-esteem, and perpetual stress. Worse still, Spot thought he was a human being. He didn't pay attention to other dogs, but only to people, who weren't thrilled when he sniffed at their bottoms. Consequently Spot's sex life was non-existent.

Spot called in the great Feng Shui master L'ong T'ung, who noticed that the sleeping basket was in the basement. Closer study showed that it lay on a line of Geopathic Stress. Spot's feeding bowl was placed in the bathroom; and his toilet area in the yard was used for growing pumpkins. This meant that the three key activities – eating, sleeping, and pooing – were dominated by human ch'i.

風
水

THE ANSWER

Master T'ung's solution was simple yet brilliant. He instructed Spot to drag his basket to the top of the house, thus raising his status in the household; to use the basement as a toilet, neutralizing the geopathic energies there; and to eat the prize pumpkins, a strategy which forced provision of a proper eating place in the kitchen. Spot is now on top of the world. He fathered six litters last year.

INTRODUCTION

ave you noticed how Feng Shui is all the rage with humans these days? They can't seem to visit the bathroom without consulting a Feng Shui Master. But they don't realize that dogs have known about Feng Shui all along; canine Feng Shui – pronounced "Fang Chewey" – is simply part of the package of being a dog, built in as standard instinctual equipment. However, it's one thing to have a nose for life in the wilderness when you're running around as dominant species, and quite another to cope with the bizarre world of modern people.

99.9% of the world's dogs now live in the weird human realm of houses, furniture, tables, chairs, and flushing toilets, which calls for massive adaptation in spatial awareness and perception of subtle energies.

WHAT THIS BOOK WILL GIVE YOU

But if you're prepared to apply yourself, this book will enable you to transform your environment. It will help you plan the best possible arrangements of your home, facilities, and territory. Its secrets will enhance your health and happiness, your career, good fortune, and love life. It bears the promise of a regular regime of exhilarating exercise, indolent leisure, and a perpetually full food bowl. And most importantly of all, it holds the key to getting your way with the humans that you live with.

THE ORIGINS OF FENG SHUI

Even human Feng Shui is a very ancient science. The first person to study it was an enigmatic Chinese sage, aptly named Hu Hsi, who lived about 3,000 years ago. But canine Feng Shui is far older still, existing as long as there have been dog-like species roaming the earth.

A NOSE FOR THE BUSINESS

Dog Feng Shui has always been a very natural business, all about developing an instinct for the energies that exist in your environment and living among them effectively. By the time of the Chow dynasty, however, it came to be studied more closely by a mysterious canine from Llasa named Apso. His teachings were later developed by the

legendary Feng Shui Master Shi-Tsu, who laid the basis for the classical form that is still used today.

The term Feng Shui literally means "wind and water," capturing the essence of the relationship between a dog, its environment, and the unfortunate influence of humans. "Water" expresses the dog's vital connection to its surroundings prompted by the leaking of fluid at every opportunity; while "Wind" evokes the unfortunate human habit of blaming canine allies for their own digestive manifestations.

THE PRINCIPLES
OF FENG SHUI

Study of the natural movements of wind and water in any environment showed the Feng Shui Masters the powerful patterns of invisible energy moving through the landscape. This universal type of energy, known as "ch'i," is the vital force which infuses all life.

The qualities and patterns of surrounding ch'i have a profound effect on the activities of dogs, people, and everything else. And so the Feng Shui of your environment can shape the course of your life – your physical and emotional well-being, your happiness and creativity, your relationships – and that most important item of all, your food supply.

IN THE FLOW

The patterns of ch'i activity are greatly affected by the form of the environment – mountains and valleys, trees

and buildings, even down to the smallest details of fittings in the home. The object of Feng Shui is to ensure that there is a healthy and balanced flow of the right kind of ch'i through your whole environment, and that it accumulates satisfactorily, yet never becomes stagnant.

Ultimately, Feng Shui provides a whole range of techniques for living more effectively and harmoniously with the energies of the natural world – despite the incredible lengths to which human beings go to make things otherwise.

APPLYING
THE PRINCIPLES

The ancient sages and masters have taught us a number of key principles by which the energies of the cosmos work. These provide profound insights into the behavior of the ch'i energies that are so crucial to a positive environment.

YIN AND YANG

First and foremost is the principle of yin and yang, or the Law of Opposites. This states that everything in the universe is

風水

characterized by one or other of these two types of energy. For instance, sometimes you feel active and dynamic and full of energy; this is an example of "yang" ch'i. Other times you're quite happy to lie around all day in a complete stupor of passive inactivity; this is "yin" ch'i at work. But your life can't be all one or all the other; harmony is a balance of both.

And it's the same with the patterns of energy in your environment. Excessively yang ch'i can occur, for instance, where hyperactive children are constantly tormenting you and kicking up a racket. Extreme yin energies often manifest themselves in human living rooms with too many easy chairs, where stagnant ch'i takes over the moment the TV is switched on.

THE FIVE ELEMENTS

The other important concept is known as the Five Elements. This is a system of subdividing or classifying types of energies that carries yin and yang a stage further.

THE CLASSICAL HUMAN SYSTEM OF FIVE ELEMENTS CONSISTS OF:

Fire   Earth   Water

Metal   Wood

This system is totally abstract, and clearly irrelevant to the dog worldview.

The canine five elements are far more down-to-earth and pertinent to the realities of practical everyday life. They are:

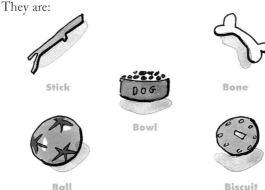

Stick

Bowl

Bone

Ball

Biscuit

Again, there should be a balance of all these types of energy, to create the most positive environment both inside and outside the home. A skilled Feng Shui practitioner will quickly be able to detect which of them is deficient or excessive where problems are being experienced. "Too many food bowls to choose from here," he may announce while sitting in contemplation in the kitchen, or "Not enough bones buried in this garden," after completing a skilled external sniff around.

DOG
DIRECTIONOLOGY

This is an important branch of Feng Shui, designed to determine which directions are favorable for certain activities and which are not. The oriental system of the Twelve Animals is a key concept in directionology.

Human study of direction and the twelve animals is extremely complex and unnecessarily hard to grasp. Dog directionology is far more sensible and practical. The other eleven animals of the canine system are the horse, cow, fox, pig, goat, sheep, cat, squirrel, chicken, rat, and mouse. There are only two basic guidelines that you need to pay attention to:

1 All twelve animals are good for chasing, in any direction.

2 The best direction to run at any time is all directions at once.

THE FOUR POINTS OF THE COMPASS

There is, however, another set of animals that you must take a lot more seriously, each with its own directional significance. These are the four metaphoric creatures that represent the four points of the compass. As a dog, you ignore their influences at your peril. They are used to indicate which quarters of a room, dwelling, or outdoor area will be most favorable, safest, and most abundant in beneficial resources.

風水

THE FOUR
ARCHETYPAL ANIMALS

SOUTH: THE RED PHOENIX

South is the most favorable direction of all to face, whether for your whole building or just a habitual lurking spot, because the bird that resides here archetypally represents the perfect prey – you can catch and eat it as many times as you want, but it still keeps coming back to life.

NORTH: THE BLACK TORTOISE

North, by contrast, is all about energies that move unbearably slowly. But north-facing rooms can still be ideal for enjoying a bit of peace and quiet, sleeping off an unusually heavy meal, or generally being degenerate.

EAST: THE GREEN DRAGON

h'i that flows from the home of this creature in the east is good for waking up and getting going. The potentially angry energy of the dragon is also excellent for annoying humans by waking them up long before their usual time.

WEST: THE WHITE TIGER

his is the one that you need to beware of. Western energies are willful, dramatic, and unpredictable – an extreme version of all that is bad about cats. Stay out of this quarter as much as possible, for the tiger ch'i lies in wait there to wreak terrible vengeance for cat-chasing done by all dogs everywhere.

THE BARK-KUA COMPASS

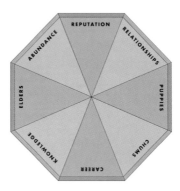

The Bark-Kua compass is a wonderful tool for dog Feng Shui. Typically, human sloppiness has corrupted the term to "Bagua."

It's an octagonal grid-like map that indicates the eight main areas of your life, and can be applied to anything from a dog-basket or kennel to a whole territory. Using it, you will be able to choose which sectors are good for which departments, or work out why certain things in your life are going wrong.

USING THE COMPASS

You have to imagine the grid as being superimposed upon the space in question, rotating until the doorway or entrance to the space lies along the bottom edge of the grid. Then you can read off which life areas correspond with which zones. The meanings of the eight sectors are shown on the Bark-Kua map.

For instance, when you want to know where food has been hidden, you could spend some time in the "Knowledge" sector of the kitchen. If you're looking for some funky action, the best part of your territory in which to wait is going to be the "Relationship" zone. All the rest of the time, you might as well hang out in the corner of "Abundance," because that's where your food ch'i is generated.

THE ART OF PLACEMENT

Every dog knows that each spot has its own unique energy quality. Sniffing this quality out is usually a quite straightforward, simple, instinctive business; however, living in a world controlled by humans complicates things for dogs – humans seem to have strong ideas on where things should be put. But if you persist with your placement choices, you'll be able to grind them down in the end. It's just a matter of being dogged about it.

WHERE TO PUT THINGS

One of the most powerful items in your Feng Shui armory is known as the Placement of Poo and Pee. For these, the best places are those where the ch'i is most stagnant and yin, which also happen to be the most out-of-the-way spots. This means that your offerings will remain exerting their positive influence longer.

Ideal placement of human artefacts, like socks, shoes, and wallets – all over the floor. The people you live with might need some help with this.

Placement of hair moltings – on rugs and furniture. Dark hairs on light-colored fabrics are particularly auspicious.

Placement of telephones: what do you need a telephone for? You're a dog.

TACTICS
OF LOCATION

The other branch of Placement is the art of where to put yourself. For instance, the ch'i which occurs just in front of doors is particularly favorable for dogs. So if you take to lying in these zones, you will receive great benefits. People coming in will trip over you, and your status in the power hierarchy of the household will rise – folks will have to take you into account a lot more.

However, this favorable ch'i is not very durable. Once you've exploited it for a while, the energies break down and humans stop falling over you. So then you'll need to move to another door-swing zone.

OTHER PLACES WITH POSITIVE DOG CH'I

Any part of the room from which you can see the doorway is excellent for destroying things.

It's good to position yourself where you can secretly watch out for your master or mistress coming home; then you can dash to the door and greet them; they become convinced you're psychic, and reward you with treats.

If the breadwinner habitually arrives home late from work and the cook gets mad about it, careful positioning can often get you an extra free meal.

Sitting behind the mailbox at delivery time offers plenty of opportunities for creative destruction.

ROOM LAYOUT

The way each room is laid out has a profound effect on the flow of ch'i. Unfortunately much of the decision-making here lies in the less-than-capable hands of humans; yet you can often still influence the situation.

FURNITURE LAYOUT

This can affect your life profoundly. Humans seem hell-bent on creating lifeless environments where all ch'i is trapped and static, so they can sit around for hours watching TV or drinking themselves silly. You will naturally prefer a more dynamic arrangement, where ch'i flows freely. Ideally, you should be able to dash through any room at breakneck speed while chasing an extremely athletic cat.

DOOR ARRANGEMENTS

As with furniture, ideal door positioning permits rapid entry, exit, and run-through. The perfect home will have the front door, back door, and all internal doors aligned. All doors should be left perpetually open – something which you may have to train your people to live with.

WHAT YOU CAN DO

Always discourage layouts which are unfavorable to you. It's amazing what a bit of judicious shredding or breaking will do to influence human decision-making.

You can also move furniture around yourself in the middle of the night.

THE GREAT OUTDOORS

Before humans came along, Feng Shui was only concerned with the consideration of outdoor energies. But nowadays, external Feng Shui must also take into account what's happening in the areas surrounding buildings.

In the great classic texts of Feng Shui, the ideal external setting for a home has a circle of high mountains in the background, a cluster of trees nearby, and a wide plain before, with a river looping round and lake directly in front. The perfect dog's version of this is exactly the same, but with the human building removed.

LIVING IN THE PRESENT MOMENT

However, as a dog today you must live in the real world. Since you're dependent on humans for almost everything, there's no point in "biting the hand that feeds you," as it were. So the utopian ideal must be tempered with a modicum of social realism. In other words, you may have to settle for that foreground plain being covered with row upon row of houses, a sweeping multi-lane expressway replacing the river, with a small ornamental pond in front; and the mountains will probably be skyscrapers downtown. Oh well, at least there'll be plenty of lamp-posts, which can be just as handy as trees.

NEAR THE HOME

on't lose heart; even in this environment of artificial ch'i, the savage spirit of the wolf still lurks below a thin veneer of civilization in even the cuddliest-seeming poodle. And you can still find energy-enhancing features in the modern landscape.

All watercourses, for instance, are basically favorable, especially ditches that are full of dirty, foul-smelling water. Even shallow puddles and expanses of mud are a positive feature, ideal for rolling around in.

The area right in front of the home is particularly

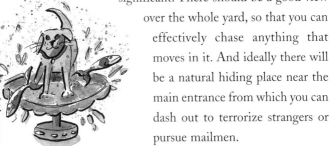

significant. There should be a good view over the whole yard, so that you can effectively chase anything that moves in it. And ideally there will be a natural hiding place near the main entrance from which you can dash out to terrorize strangers or pursue mailmen.

OVER THE GARDEN WALL

Generally speaking, high walls or fences create bad Feng Shui, blocking the flow of ch'i and limiting your constitutional right of freedom to roam. However, there are ways of exploiting this. For instance, if you're a wimp you can run up and down all day behind a fence, barking like crazy at anything that goes by, as if to let them know they're really lucky the fence is there.

FURTHER AFIELD

ere, the most auspicious ch'i lies in landscapes where you can connect with your ancestral energies and run with the pack. Ideal outdoor Feng Shui calls for a clear distance in each direction that can be sprinted non-stop in half a day. As a rough guide, this means:

for a fit Rotweiller, thirty-seven miles each way;

for a spoilt, overfed Chihuahua, about twenty-nine square yards.

There should be an adequate provision of trees or other vertical objects, evenly spaced out at thirty-pace intervals. Plenty of sheep, cows, and rabbits will also enhance landscape ch'i.

LINES OF CH'I

"Secret Arrows" are very dangerous. These are pathways of "sha" or unhealthy ch'i, created by anything that creates a perfectly straight line, which of course means most things made by humans. Fortunately secret arrows can be rendered safe by bending, breaking, chewing, or otherwise reducing the straightness of the offending features.

Better still, you can create positive arrows of your own. The best way of doing this is by burying Secret Wiggly Lines of tasty bones underground.

Watch out for natural "power points" in the yard. These are usually indicated by the presence of the gardener's most prized plants. Favor these with your sacred "gifts to the ground" (i.e. poo).

Seek out "ley lines", and lay on them.

GOOD FENG SHUI

You can tell from your own state if you're living in a setting that has good Feng Shui. Your coat will be glossy, and your eyes bright. You catch everything you chase. Your tail-wag is in overdrive all the time. No matter how much you've eaten, you always fancy a bit more. Your mouth has that true "dog-breath" tang. When you're out exercising your owner, your ratio of how-far-you-run to how-far-they-walk is up around a hundred. These are the effects of living in an ideal energy field.

CLUTTER

In human Feng Shui, something called "space clearing" is very big at the moment; "clutter" is the new C-word, and it's on everyone's lips. They've got it completely the wrong way round; they think clutter is bad. Yet to the enlightened dog, a high clutter factor is crucial to positive ch'i flow and overall vitality. But don't worry about human efforts in this direction – the universe is on your side. Cosmic energies dictate that clutter is automatically self-reinstating, and that attempts at space-clearing are of only fleeting effect. Clutter, then is really good Feng Shui.

OTHER
POSITIVE FEATURES

he presence of children is usually an indication of positive Feng Shui; they are infinitely more abundant in ch'i and enthusiasm, and far more fun than their morbid adult counterparts. However, certain young specimens can be a pain in the rear end. On the plus side, many kids contribute to the positive flow of energies by giving you unscheduled extra food, including the food that has the most potent ch'i of all – prime scraps from the human plate.

風
水

Color is another important aspect of your surrounding energy field. Ideally, everything in the home – walls and ceilings, woodwork, fixtures and fittings, ornaments, and utensils – should be colored brown, the most favourable color in the dog spectrum. However, this color scheme isn't always first choice among humans. Yet all is not lost – bear in mind that almost any colored surface tends to revert to a harmonious grayish-brown when enough dirt and grime is applied to it. No doubt you can find ways to assist in this beneficial process.

BAD FENG SHUI

Just as surely as with good Feng Shui, the effects of negative energies will reveal themselves unmistakably in your own life state.

SIGNS AND SYMPTOMS

When there's bad Feng Shui, you're tired all day, but can't sleep even at night. Your tail feels like it's made of lead. Your coat becomes dull, but you don't even want to get covered in mud. You hide behind a sofa when you hear

風水

strange noises at night. Word gets around to local cats that they can wash themselves right under your nose and get away with it. You experience the dark night of the soul in the middle of the afternoon. Then it gets really bad - you don't even want to eat. That's when you know you've got to do something.

As you know, dogs are basically irrepressibly optimistic creatures that can accommodate any amount of obnoxious influence from humans, but are extremely sensitive to environmental factors. So if the description above sounds like you, check out whether any of the following features exist in your situation.

BAD FENG SHUI
FEATURES

high incidence of cats is one of the worst possible Feng Shui influences; buildings catering for them have an even more powerful concentration of negative ch'i. This includes cat hotels and motels, breeding establishments, houses where several cats live, and homes where the cat rules the roost – in practice this means most of them. The only effective remedy is to chase these offending influences out of town.

DOGGED BY YOUR PAST

Everything that has happened in the past leaves an imprinted energy pattern, sometimes with extremely negative effects. Perhaps the worst scenario here is when a house has "hungry ghosts" – the spirits of dogs who died without having recently eaten. Previous canine residents can also exert a harmful influence if your owners liked them more than you, and keep their pictures around the place. The solution is to knock the pictures off the wall and bury them in the yard.

OTHER SITUATIONS THAT POSSESS STRONG NEGATIVE CH'I INCLUDE:

Households where the dog is a "house pet" and can never go out.

Any building that has a dog hitch outside.

Veterinary premises. Don't even think about going there; you'll probably come back incomplete – if indeed you come back at all.

CURES
AND REMEDIES

ures and remedies are what to resort to when you've got a bad Feng Shui situation, and you really wish to quickly change the existing ch'i patterns.

Humans use rather strange devices for this, such as mirrors, crystals, wind-chimes, and plants in huge pots. These are of little real value – except perhaps the plant pots, when you're caught short and can't be bothered going outside. Dog remedies are far more practical and down-to-earth. Here are a few suggestions.

Persuade your owner to get an aquarium, one of the most powerful cures for stagnant ch'i. But make sure it's stocked with dogfish; catfish are clearly a no-no.

Scents can be potent enhancers of positive energies. Leave them everywhere.

Sound is effective too. When ch'i gets "stuck," clear it with loud and persistent barking.

Dribbling and soaking things with saliva also enhances the energies of negatively charged objects.

When a stronger cure is required, make life miserable for your owners until they move to a preferable situation.

If even that fails, run away and hang around a house that has really good Feng Shui, looking all cute, forlorn, and homeless, until you get taken in.

ROMANCE AND
RELATIONSHIPS

Feng Shui energies can have a powerful effect on your love life. But here too your needs can be very different from those of your human co-occupants.

Human beings are incredibly repressed about their sexual activity, so they favor having plenty of dark, secret corners to do it in. This naturally creates a great deal of excessively yin and stagnant ch'i.

They also play hard-to-get, pretend they don't want it when they do, and generally make things very difficult. No wonder they lack *joie-de-vivre*.

風水

DOG DELIGHT

Dogs, by contrast, are delighted to act out their strongest reproductive instincts in the wide open spaces, where the ch'i flows free and strong - "letting it all hang out," as the humans might say. Dogs have none of the complicated relationship problems that humans seem to excel at.

Here is a list of places that have good Feng Shui for canine romance-and-relationship activities. You will find that it's really very simple.

For finding a partner – anywhere.

For licking your genitals – anywhere.

For having sex – anywhere and everywhere.

There is one type of environment, however, that has deadlier romance Feng Shui than any other. If you find yourself suddenly being put in a basket one day around the age of six to nine months and taken away, you're probably on your way there.

DOG DOCTOR ▷

HEALTH
AND HAPPINESS

The Feng Shui in your home will also have a profound effect on your physical, mental, and emotional well-being. Way ahead of all other factors, of course, is food; a dog's health and happiness begins and ends with food ch'i. Having plenty of food lying around all the time is the number one positive-energy criterion.

Remember also that human food is more highly charged with healthful ch'i than what is gotten from a can and put in your bowl. So make sure that you are on hand at human mealtimes, especially if there are children in your house.

YOUR OWN FENG SHUI

Personal Feng Shui is also important. Personal ch'i can be enhanced by a modest amount of self-grooming, licking, and so on, but is diminished by the excessive shampooing, preening, and professional grooming that humans lavish on the more unfortunate pedigree breeds.

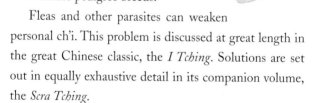

Fleas and other parasites can weaken personal ch'i. This problem is discussed at great length in the great Chinese classic, the *I Tching*. Solutions are set out in equally exhaustive detail in its companion volume, the *Scra Tching*.

Finally, bear in mind that neurotic human concern about your appearance and well-being can have its advantages. So once in a while you might want to feign illness, look miserable, or even refuse food, when you need to swing things your way.

CAREER DEVELOPMENT

Career is something that people don't even think dogs have; that's because their only concern in life is to be paranoidly goal-oriented and neurotically stressed-out all the time. Dog career development is based on far more sensible ideals. Life is for living in the here and now; if something isn't worth doing this second, forget it; in fact, a key part of life is doing nothing at all. The longest-term concern is when the next walk will happen and where the next meal is coming from.

IT'S IN THE AIR

The most relevant branch of Feng Shui here relates to the changing patterns of atmospheric ch'i over time, and how to choose favorable timing for different actions and activities. Humans go to ridiculous extremes to do this, consulting endless almanacs and mystics. But dogs exercise a far more pragmatic approach, mostly by sniffing the air. For instance, when you sense that your master or mistress is in a particularly good mood, it's an auspicious occasion to beg for treats and negotiate for concessions. But when the atmosphere is pervaded by foul temper, make yourself scarce.

Any day, though, is auspicious for walks, over-eating, fighting, stealing things, and running around with a bunch of mates looking for trouble.

COPING
WITH HUMANS

OBEDIENCE CLASS

The single greatest source of negative energies is people. Here are some tips for reducing their damaging influence.

It's vital to establish from the start that you are merely tolerating their presence in your home; training or "socializing" your humans is therefore a top priority. Most humans seem to have got this completely the wrong way round; they think that they are training you. Some even have the bizarre idea that they can become some sort of "top dog," when they aren't any kind of dog at all.

風
水

HINTS AND TIPS

The best strategy is to humor them – let them go on thinking they're in charge, permit a few small and unimportant concessions, but make sure you get your way in really major matters. In troublesome cases, you may need to send them to obedience classes.

Reinforce their behavior when it positively affects your environment, by so-called "good dog" behavior – loyalty, affection, and all that nonsense.

Discourage their poor decisions by a campaign of disobedience, stealing, playing obscenely with visitors' legs, and pretending (noisily) that there's an intruder breaking in during the night.

Use sneakiness, tantrums, sulking, fussy eating, and general manipulativeness as and when required.

RITUALS AND PROCEDURES

Once in a while you're sure to encounter a negative ch'i situation which no amount of cures, remedies, or manipulation of humans can change. For instance, there might be an extremely powerful and unscarable feline presence residing very close to your sleeping area.

MAKING MAGIC

In this kind of case the traditional Feng Shui approach is the use of potent magical rituals to dispel the negative energies. Human versions of these are absurdly complex

風
水

and superstitious – like building a shrine, creating a lot of smoke to "purify" the atmosphere, or chanting lots of strange utterances. Sometimes the shrines are okay, because they often have bits of food on them.

Dog rituals for solving intractable energy problems are simplicity itself, and can be adapted to almost any situation. Here are some examples of procedures to use at the place where negative ch'i is concentrated:

Roll over on your back and squirm around a lot.

Jump up and down a great deal, while barking.

Walk around in a circle three times and then fall asleep on the spot for the rest of the day. On top of the cat in this case – that's a good example of adapting the method to individual circumstance.

POWER PLACES

There are certain places on the Earth's surface that are supercharged with great amounts of strong and positive ch'i. These are known in Feng Shui as Power Places.

You can tell when you're near one of these — the hair rises on your neck, you feel incredible surges of energy, and

your tail-wag goes into involuntary hyper-drive. Some of these places inherently possess particularly powerful earth forces, while in others the ch'i has become concentrated by ancient usage and sacred events.

The most important types of Power Place are crossings of major ley lines, ancient burial mounds, traditional sites of tribal dog battles, and circles of standing stones that have been used from time immemorial for sacred passing-of-water ceremonies. There are also some mini-power-places in your home. These include:

In front of the fire.

By the front door.

Anywhere that's really smelly.

Visiting Power Places is excellent for developing personal power, power over other dogs or power over people – or just power napping. But the greatest benefit is gained by making a pilgrimage to one of the world's great Power Places; you'll find these listed in the cult book, *Chariots of the Dogs*. Most celebrated are the burial places of Lassie, Mount Kaileash in Tibet, and the greatest of them all – Bonehenge.

No animals have
been harmed in the writing
of this book.

The author can be contacted
on
e-mail gerry@pavilion.co.uk

This book is dedicated to Lik-Yu, the affectionate Pekingese sage who taught me so much.

In a past life, Gerry Maguire Thompson was a Great Dane/Chihuahua cross-breed.